Blue Butterfly

Amia Virena Brown

BookLeaf
Publishing

Presentation by *BookLeaf Publishing*

Web: www.bookleafpub.com

E-mail: info@bookleafpub.com

ISBN: 9789357214490

First edition 2023

*To everyone who has a broken heart that still
beats and wants to find love.*

ACKNOWLEDGEMENT

I would first like to thank God for holding onto me and not letting me give up on those many nights when I just wanted to quit. I appreciate your love for me. Next, I would like to thank my family for loving me and being supportive of my dreams. Finally, I want to thank the staff at the Covenant House California for giving me a chance to be myself and believing in my story when I didn't. Thank you all.

PREFACE

When I was a teen, I saw a blue and black butterfly waiting for me when I was upset one day and walking down my parents' driveway. I greeted the butterfly and said "goodbye" before leaving and the butterfly flew away. I knew then that I had seen an angel and that God was letting me know that He loved me. This book is named after that moment and is inspired by the ups and downs I have with God, myself, and others, as I try to navigate life.

Intro

It sucks when you want to die
but have to stay alive
because you couldn't do anything even if you
tried your hardest
and God above seems the farthest away

A broken heart is never truly restored
and bullets in the brain just stay and fester
They're still around even when the pain
becomes lesser
How did my life end up like this?

On meds that stabilize
but comes at a price
A heavy, unhealthy price
but still nothing seems alright
How did depression go to psychosis and more
severe things?
I guess that's the price when it goes untreated

It's not like this always
it just gets bad sometimes
One day I'm okay
and the next I can't stop crying

I just want to feel better and loved
in a world that's on fire
but I don't know where to start
Church?
Therapy?
Some advice from mom?
Who knows

All I know is that I'm not coughing or sneezing
or struggling to breathe
but I've got a pain that's insane and it astonishes
me that I'm still standing

Welcome to My Testimony
my name is Amia
and you, dear reader,
are in for a hell of a ride

Little Me/Big Me

Little Me was so free
she was kinda sassy
and kinda mean
she had a lot of talent
and she had a lot of faith
I guess I'm still waiting for
her to come back one day

Big Me still has the talent
but the confidence is gone
Big Me is learning to love
But Big Me has kindness and compassion
and she cares so much
Big Me has experience and stories to tell
Big Me is sad but she is doing well

Little Me was so free
and Big Me wants to be
there are some things they can learn from each
other
Though Little Me isn't here,
Big Me carries her in her heart
and is finishing what she started
This crazy life we've been put in
we've gotta finish it 'til the end

The child inside isn't here
but there's still room to grow
We've got people to see
and we've got places to go
We've got to learn to love

Little Me had a spark that the world put out
But Big Me knows where to go
to get a flame that never dies
but she doesn't trust anymore;
something she's got to learn to do

Little Me, Big Me,
allow me to introduce you
you both are Amia
just different signs of different times
you could learn from one another
so when an older me comes, she'll be a little
wiser

Though I long for aspects of the past,
life keeps going forward
I guess I should move on
it's just, I loved her
The person I was as a little girl was so beautiful
and now she's gone
But as life keeps going,
there's still more time to grow

Lost in the Cosmos

I like the idea of being lost in the cosmos
Just a single soul, alone,
inside an infinitely enormous
and ever-growing canvas of stars and galaxies,
beautifully painted with lights of all colors and
kinds

I want to be lost in the cosmos,
Defying Gravity
and traveling through space, alone and free
Unknown to the universe, somewhere where no
one can find me
A tiny soul exploring for eternity
With a whole lot of stories to make
or maybe I can just float around and be easy
Lost in the Cosmos,
That's where I want to be

Sorry

Sorry doesn't mean anything
to someone you don't know
Who only saw you for a moment
and now feels hurt

Hurt people hurt people
still, it doesn't excuse
atrocities from the mouth
and words that attack

A moment of passion
It felt right in the moment
But now I regret it
And now, I look like a monster
Or at least someone to pass up
When looking for a relationship

He's long gone
But I still hold on
to that moment that didn't mean anything to me
but meant everything to him

Sorry A,
I was frustrated
but that's still not an excuse
to say hurtful things to you

I guess I've been desensitized
to cruelty and unloving nature
Still, it's no excuse
for lashing out

You're long gone
don't know if you'll ever come back around
First impressions are important I guess
and I blew it

Then I left
maybe you were willing to hold on
But I'm not ready for love
I won't even accept God's

But maybe one day,
this anger will be released
'Till then I'll bathe in my regret
and wish we could redo our first meet

You and Me

Hand in hand, you and me
This love will last forever
You and me, get older together

Hand in hand, you and me
Never letting go
We've got history

Though demons haunt,
they're there when no one else is
Though demons haunt,
they're there when the day ends

Never letting go, you and me
Hand in hand, we've got history

We've got history

Remember when we got lost in the city?
Walking through the streets, wandering
endlessly

Remember when we got committed?
Finally able to say what was hurting

Remember when we got on that bus?
Scared for the future, the two of us

Just the two of us

I remember when you held me underwater
My favorite song played on my phone
I felt at peace but it wasn't the end of me

I remember when you inspired my best art
But you told me to throw it away
It wasn't worth trying to stay

There are many things I remember

Like the fear you put in me
if I ever were to leave
Or the scars you painted on my skin
Or the way you kept me from my kin
Or how you saw the worse in everyone

Including me

I remember how you kept me from God
and how you made not believe

Hand in hand, you and me

Though demons haunt

Though demons haunt

You were a friend
but now you're not

Now I've grown and I know

Hand lets go, you I leave
The love is gone
No more history
You and me
We're over

I walk forward, you stay behind
Though the memories still haunt my mind
It's over

We're over

Simple Sign of Love

I wear it always
I will for years to come
I remember what you did
that simple sign of love

Though you didn't know all of me
you looked at me without judgement
And I regret not keeping in touch

But I remember what you did
the day I left
that simple sign of love
I will carry it with me

I'm sorry I didn't wear it right away
because I didn't believe
that He was real
But now I know
He's the only place love comes from

Thank you for loving me
I will do my best to carry on the legacy
and show others what it means to be loved and
not judged

That simple sign of love
I never take it off
That simple sign of love
I carry it in my heart
And that good memory in my mind
washes away the shame and hate from the
previous days

I believe some things happen for a reason
and God teaches in many ways

A cross necklace
my simple sign of love
Though it's small it carries a lot
It is the symbol of the Son
who died because He loves
That simple sign of love

Tears from a Sister

Tears from my sister are hard to see
A hospital gown,
this time it's not me
Tears from a sister

Skin and bone
skinny as can be
unhealthy proportions
the weight of beauty
crushes

Tears from a sister
we were almost out the door
They wanted to get back at us
so they feigned concern

We held each other
like it was the end of the world
I knew she was going to go through hell
I could just tell

How can they take away someone's rights like
that?
Say they're not of sound mind
and force treatment?

In a place where people are mistreated?
She's of sound mind
Just not body
The weight of beauty

They take her away
I have to leave
Tears of a sister
This time I can't believe
what's happening

Only on Earth does tragedy strike
Only on Earth, where the worse of humanity
prevails
This doesn't happen in Heaven
It seems like an experience from Hell

Tears for my sister
A fist in the air
No longer will injustice reign

I wake up, somewhat relieved
But remember the skin and bone
the weight of beauty
still remains
The dream had some truth

Well wishes for my sister
hope the stress doesn't get the best of her

Well wishes for my sister
Hope she finds the person of her dreams
and becomes the mother she's always wanted to
be

I love you, sister
You are my friend
and I think of you every day
Hoping it gets better
for you sister

I hope you get the world and more

Love,

 Your sister

I'm Okay

Happiness is a lie
A phrase I once believed to be true
Depression makes you believe things
that you never knew was in your mind

Happiness, a lie?

Why should I strive so hard to get it?
Shouldn't it come naturally?
Why do all these gurus and motivational
speakers
have all the secrets?

Happiness
It feels like a tall tale to me
Maybe because this world makes it so
unbearable to be

I'm better now
then when I first exclaimed it
but this feeling I feel isn't happiness
it's content

I'm content
I'm okay

I don't know if I'll ever be "happy" again
To me, that feeling describes me as a kid
Playing with toys and too unaware of what
others thought
Shielded from the sadness that was in my
parents' home

Happiness. A lie
My feel-good feelings are gone

Though depression no longer has his hands
around my throat
And I no longer crave for death like humans do
water
I still think there is some truth to what my sad
mind said

I think happiness, as society puts it, is a lie
It's not a choice
It's a feeling

A positive mindset won't stop the storm from
coming
or blowing you this way and that
So, I don't strive to be happy
It's just not in my nature
I'm okay with being okay
You're free to disagree with me
this is just how I survive

I don't want to achieve the impossible
What I've done already is remarkable
Depression no longer has his hands around my
throat
He no longer holds me underwater
Or gets me to hold a knife to my skin
I'm not sad all the time anymore
and I see that as a win

I'll always remember my affair with death
and how I longed to be with her
I still remember how "happy" she made me feel
But it's over between me and her, you see
and I no longer strive to be happy
I'm okay with being okay

I don't need the world
I just need to not hurt
so happiness, as I know it, is dead to me
I'm content with just being
Depression no longer has his hands around my
throat
That is something!

I know as the years go by,
I'll yet again change my outlook on life
But for now, as a twenty-something-year-old,
I will let myself know that I'm proud that I let go

of my affair with death
No, I didn't do it by myself
God intervened
and I knew I was defeated
How I feel about it, I still don't know
But at least I knew how to roll with the punches

I'm not sad
I'm damn sure not happy
I'm okay with being okay
And that's worth something

Believe

I wait and I wait
for something I'm not sure about
I wait and I wait
All the while, I am filled with doubt

I'm not sure if I'm still waiting
I kind of left the promise behind
but inside I'm still hoping
that it's true

A second chance at life
A dream come true
An impossible promise
just me and you

But what if I'm only dreaming?
What if it was never real from the start?
What if I don't know what I'm talking about?
What if it wasn't a promise from God?

But how I wish I could believe
Me and you - a reality
How I wish I wasn't fooled so easily
How I wish my faith was stronger
and my brain a little less faulty

But wouldn't it be so amazing
if it were to come true
and to everyone who ever doubted me,
I get to say "I told you"

Nothing's impossible for God
so why can't I believe
when He says "you'll get what you dreamed"?

I wish I was a better Christian
I wish I was stronger in faith
They say it's not over until God says
so maybe I can still turn it around
and trust my heart more than my faulty brain
and maybe just maybe pray

Tell God how I'm feeling and that I need aid
I don't know what's real sometimes
and that can get tricky
Still, I know He's up to something
I just need to believe it's for my good
and get rid of the parasites and naysayers
that never understood
I guess I just gotta believe
and establish a stronger faith connection
so the devil can't destroy what is my blessing

I wonder if God is waiting for me to come to
Him
I know a blessing isn't a transaction
There's something for me to learn
in the midst of all this confusion
I want to open my eyes and see the real from the
illusion

Still, it's hard for me to pray
I can't do it like I used to
something was destroyed over the years of
storms
and I don't know how to rekindle that fire inside
Still, I want to open my eyes
and believe in something greater than this world
get that faith back that I had as a little girl

and Believe

Little Angels

I turn on the news to see
yet another tragedy
A child that was abused
A child that was killed
A child that never knew what love was

Why is it so easy for some
to get pregnant and then bring that child home
to a house of horrors and a life of pain?
All the while others are trying in vain
for a little one to love

Why is it that CPS has yet again dropped the
ball?
So many reported about what was going on
yet the child remained in the home
When is it enough?
When will these tragedies stop?

Broken spine
Boiled alive
Beheaded
Abandoned on the road and left to die
These poor children; never given a chance at life

Mental illness
Drugs
Never wanted to be a parent
Who knows
These deplorable people; now rotting in a prison
cell
No amount of "justice" can undo what they did

At least the babies are living a better life in
Heaven
but why did they have to suffer so?
Such a short life
So much abuse they endured
I wish I knew the cure

All I know is to report any incident I witness
because these little kids are voiceless
and they need someone looking out for them
You and I can be the solution
and make sure these kids have a loving home
I know we can't save everyone
but we can try to give these little angels a better
life

(Inspired by the YouTube Channel 'The Misery
Machine')

The Monster

Heart
Skin
Blood
Brains
My monster is on the table still
Everyone around me thinks I'm ill
But I'm on a mission

Roof open
Lightning coming
Can't wait for the heart to beat
Can't wait to see these dead things
come to life

Roof open
Lightning... none
I thought it was a thunderstorm
Smell is rotten
I feel like puking
What was I thinking?

BOOM!
Thunder at last!
Now it's time for the
ZAP!

I fall to the floor
I'm not alive anymore
I float up toward a light
but I'm not ready to say goodbye
so I find a new body
I guess the monster is me

Heart beating
Skin moving
Blood pumping
Brains working
Body hurting
I get off this cold table
I look in the mirror
I scream
I look horrifying
The life of a mad scientist

A Princess and A Witch

The princess in the tower
wants to watch the world burn
She breathes fire
and declares it's their turn
to feel trapped

The princess killed the dragon
and tore down the walls
Now she's on a rampage
and has contempt for all!

Run everyone! Run
Her heart's as black as coal
Run everyone! Run
She won't stop 'till she reaches her goal

Fire everywhere
Nowhere to go
We're at the end of the world
save us, someone!

The witch in the forest
heard the screams of the town
She flew over to the chaos
and saw it all burn down

The princess had them cornered
there was nowhere for them to go
Until the witch cast a spell
to end the reign of the wicked woman
The princess lost her fire and fell to the ground

The people cheered the witch
and went after the princess
but they both disappeared
into the night

When the princess came to
she saw the witch and became frightened
but the witch showed her mercy and let her go
"Wickedness doesn't pay," the witch said; I
should know
"Now go, live your life. You're no longer bound"

The princess took off her crown
and went forward through the forest
The witch went back to her cottage
but the princess came back and asked the witch
"Would you like an apprentice?"

Sting of Shame

 You're wrong about me
making assumptions and whispering
to one another
about what she said that she said that he said that
I said
It's unbelievable!

Still, I feel the sting of shame
that you all associated with my name
But you're wrong about me
and I wish I could've spoken up for myself
but my tongue always becomes severed
in the middle of battle
so I'm stuck with another shitty memory

Fuck all of you for bullying me
and fuck that EMT for seeing the worse in me
and insulting me when I needed help
people will let you down every time you put
your faith in them
some of the things they do are straight-up evil
and then they try to justify it by blaming me
yeah, I made mistakes but does that call for
bullying?

You may have gotten the best of me a year ago
but I know what I said and didn't say
and I am so sick of feeling shame
when I had no reason to
I'm the so-called "crazy" one but I never set out
to intentionally hurt anyone
yet you did
but I get punished for experiencing psychosis?
And don't you dare tell me to "get over it"
It was a bitter taste of injustice
and it was wrong

But that's just how the story goes sometimes
you get treated badly and then you just have to
deal with it
I wish I could be a little more uplifting but that
would be lying
Sometimes you have to write to keep from
crying
but then you cry anyways

It's days like these that make me wish I could
leave it all behind
and not have to deal with this life
It's weeks like those that make me so angry
but I can't do anything about it

I guess one day I might come to terms with it
but not today

They were wrong
but what can I do about that?

I am angry
and I am sad
and I have no outlet
which is a recipe for disaster
The memories replay
and still, I feel that sting of shame

Some Bridges

I lock you away behind a door I never intend to
open
I hear you bang and plead to be let out
But I know you're dangerous
so, I try to drown out your shouts

I threw away the key
but still, your spirits aren't broken
and then someone wrongs me
and the devil has awoken

You break down that door
and come to my aid
but your fire is too hot sometimes
so you make people afraid

And then comes the regret
Words I wish I never said
Tears falling down cheeks
I let you get the best of me

Why is it that I'm either weak or mean?
I can't find a common ground with myself
or the anger that's built up over the years
it's like a volcano buried under a pile of snow

my anger is drowned out by the cold of
numbness and nihilistic feelings
until I feel my heart beating
and my voice shaking
and then I feel the fire awakening
and someone gets burned

I want to learn to manage it
I guess therapy would do me some good
but I won't let anyone it yet
because my feelings are never understood

Still, I long for that outlet
that place where I can let it all out
and not be judged when I start to shout
and cry and punch the wall and ask why
people push me to this point
My brain remains out of order
but my soul will always be unbroken

It's time for you and me to have a conversation
so we don't burn it all down
some bridges lead to a better place
so it's time we cross them
instead of going in circles, around and around

Some bridges lead to a better place
so let's see where it takes us

My Testimony

It's not normal
so why is it being treated as so?
Abuse is abuse
whether physical or verbal
I'm so sick of begging for validity
so I wrote and I felt free

It may not be newsworthy
but it's my story
No one can say it's worthless
No one should be silenced for speaking up
about the people that hurt them

Things may be better now
but I'll never get back that time as a child
that time when I felt safe
instead of feeling compelled to run away
that time when I wasn't always crying or
wishing I could die young

You yelled at me all the time
you never listened when I told you what was
hurting
you mocked me for feeling suicidal
and you tried to control every part of my life

you may be better now but you were shitty to me
as a child
and I will never forget that

It was abuse
and there is no excuse that anyone can make up
for you
that will make me say it wasn't true
and I was just overreacting
but when I find myself switching personalities
and reliving trauma in the shower
that's all the confirmation I need
so fuck outside validity
I know what is true for me

And I can't care what they'll say about me
because they don't know All of Me
and when I realize that truth
that sting of shame becomes a little smaller
and I stand a little taller

Next time, I will look them in the eyes
and speak what's on my mind
and stop trying to be so damn nice
to assholes that don't give a fuck about me
It's about time I get some fight in me
and stop caring about outside validity
and start sharing my testimony
so I can help others like me

Autistic and Dissociative and Depressed, Black,
White, all kids, women, men, people who were
silenced and wanted their stories to end but
God had other plans and now they're in the in
between
Not really wanting to stay but knowing they
can't leave just yet
because they know their work on Earth isn't
done

I know I'm not the only one
who's somewhat suicidal and questioning their
Christianity
but somehow holding onto faith in God
because they've seen the absolute worst of
humanity

As you read my poems, you get just a piece of
the story
but I promise you there's more of my testimony

Some parts are in this book
others to be announced
I know there was some purpose to my pain
and I'm not living in vain
and one day, it will all make sense
but until then

This is my testimony

One Day

Maybe one day it'll be me
as a bride, walking down the aisle in a beautiful
dress
meeting my one true love
exchanging vows and letting everyone know
this is who I want to spend my life with

I want to be optimistic and believe that I can be
a good wife for somebody
I just got to stop pushing everyone away
and cutting flowers before they bloom

I've had a long line of potential lovers
and through my actions, the love was cut off
I just didn't want to get stuck in a bad
relationship
but I judged it all too soon
and walked away before anything could develop
Yeah, when it comes to love, I'm kind of a
screw-up
still, that doesn't stop me from wishing
I could be the one in the white dress

In my mind, I have a wife
and she's beautiful and kind

and she's proud to be herself
and she makes me want to be a better person

I see us at the altar, both wearing dresses
quoting our favorite love songs for vows
and exchanging rings
Then, we dance and take pictures and be
unapologetically gay
on our special day

In my mind, I give love a shot
In my heart, that is what I want
to love and be loved by the one true
I pray one day it will be me and you

Seventeen

I remember what it was like to be seventeen
For me, it meant being depressed and rebellious
and sick of everyone's shit
and downplaying my accomplishments

It meant running away over and over again
and wanting to take on the world
Wanting to be an adult but still being a little girl

I remember what it felt like to be seventeen
to act out and feel a little bit free
from the stuff that weighed me down
it was a feeling like no other

Of course, that's when the hospitalizations
started
and cutting off contact with my family
and not being able to decide whether I loved or
hated them
and then came the meds and insomnia and the
suicidal feelings
and all the while hearing what people were
whispering about me

It was a tough time and I'm better at
twenty-three,
but what a time it was to be seventeen!

I remember those late nights when I couldn't
sleep
and my mom stayed up worried about me
I remember being so angry at God
for making me stay alive
I still get angry sometimes
but I at least have something forward to look to
now:

A career in the arts and a family to make
and maybe a debut on Broadway
who knows what life will bring
I'm just glad God didn't give up on me
and now I will not give up on myself

Who knows where life will bring me
I'm excited to see what twists and turns are in
store
I finally see a future
that my seventeen-year-old self never did

I've come a long way
and I'm happy it wasn't the end of the road
before
I have no idea how much longer I have

but I do know that I want to spend it doing the
things I love

I've got dreams to see come true
and places to be
I've got people to see
I've got things to do
and I'm going to spend my time doing the things
I love

Like singing and dancing and playing with my
dogs
I learned some things at seventeen
but I'm glad I made it to twenty-three
and hopefully, I'll do the things we've been
dreaming of

Baby Girl, we didn't lose, we won!
So, let's have some fun!
and live out the rest of this story in all its glory
and see what plans God has for us.

My Brother

Bro Bro, Buddy, Joshie, Best Friend
these are the names I give to my brother
who is a Godsend
Brother, I love you and wish you all the best in
life
I know sometimes you struggle, but trust me,
it'll be alright

God has so much in store for you
so it's okay if it's not all figured out
The important thing is that you enjoy the
journey
and in the unenjoyable parts, you learn
something

I love you, brother, and I want the world for you
You always know how to cheer me up
and come to the rescue

I know I can be a pain sometimes and
I promise I'll do better
I just thank God for you
because with you, any storm I can weather

Joshbo, Bud, Joshua, my friend

You are someone I cannot live without
and I'm with you 'til the end

I love you, Josh

Paw Prints On My Heart

Paw prints on my heart
left behind by all my furry friends
some are still with me and some not
but they are not forgotten

Snowball, Avalanche, Jazzy, Angel, Preacher,
King and Kilo
I love you all dearly
I hope my kisses and my hugs
filled you all with love
I hope the toys and the blankets
let you know how much you are appreciated

I know you can't understand all my words
but hopefully you will remember my smile and
my touch
I know you can't read this poem
but I want to express how much I love you all

You buddies are the best and you've shown me
unconditional love
The kind of love that comes from God above
For the ones that have went on to Heaven
please wait for me at the Rainbow Bridge
and for the ones I have,

I promise I will cherish every moment

Every time you howl at an ambulance siren
or beg for food
or rip something up,
I'll be glad I have you

I might get frustrated sometimes
but it'll be alright
nothing beats time with you two,
King and Kilo
I love you buddies!
You are a part of me
and I am thankful for you
and the paw prints you left on my heart

Beloved

Heart beating, voice shaking,
eyes avoiding the conversation
Low self-esteem comes in many forms
I want it to be a memory
in the back of my mind
as I do my thing on stage and smile

I want to sing so loud and proud
and dance like I'm not self conscious
I want to talk to someone without wondering
what they think of me
I want to not look
when I hear someone whispering; thinking
they're dog mouthing a stranger
I want to stand up for myself when people treat
me bad
I want to be unapologetically me
Is that too hard to dream?

I wish I could look in the mirror and be happy
with who I see
Not how I look, but all of me
How I laugh, what I like to do, my little habits,
and what I think
I wish other people didn't get the best of me

I wish I could be Amia and not care who doesn't
like Amia
I wish I wasn't in my head so much
I wish I could love who I am
through and through

I should
I mean, why shouldn't I be loved?
Why should I have to believe the lies of people
who didn't know anything about me?
People who made me feel less than?
People who really don't matter?

Why should I be afraid of small minded people?
People who won't give me the time of day?
It's not okay.

I should say "I am"
I heard there is power in affirmations

So

I am lovable
I am intelligent
I am talented
I am good

I am brave

I am strong
I am forgiven
and I must learn to love as I should

I know it's not a one and done
I can't declare it and it happens just like that
Especially since I've fallen out of love with life
and myself
But I must learn and keep learning to be well
and that includes thinking healthy thoughts of
me
I'm not there yet but this is the beginning

I want to love Amia again
I want us to have some fun
and I want us to find love
I want us to know who we are
and reach for the stars

Because I deserve to be loved
and treated right
and not have to fight to have good things come
my way
I'm making my one day today

I must love Amia/ me
like I want to be loved
Of course the only true love comes from God
above

I don't love right now
but maybe things will change
After all, God knew what he was doing when He
gave me this name.

Blue Butterfly

Blue butterfly, I miss seeing you
You reminded me that everything was alright
and that someone was looking out for me
someone still is and His name is Jesus

I just wish I wasn't so sad or angry
you know, I don't want to be
I want to live in love and God's truth
I want to get back the faith I had as a youth

Blue butterfly,
I know you know how much I loved God
and how I was a Christian with pride
I remember getting up and looking forward to
my devotion
and how I was filled will so much emotion when
I thought about Heaven and angels and my
Savior who loves me
Now, I'm sad and angry, but I don't want to be

I want that love back as well as the appreciation
I had
I want to love again and live like I never have
I want things to be different

Blue butterfly,
will it be alright if I trusted God with all my life?
If I just allowed Him to come in
and make the changes that need to happen?
I don't really know how to do that,
but maybe you could show me the way?

I remember how loved I felt
when I saw you

God loves me and that's true
I remember how exciting it was
and how good it felt to be seen
and I remember how God showed me that Jesus
is real

Blue butterfly,
I guess I just need more time
to be okay with this
to be okay with being God's and living
according to His will
I know He wants the best for me
I just want to be free
I know with God, I still can be
but I'm having a hard time believing
and letting go of how it used to be
before you showed up and let me know
that what I was taught is real
I'm just telling you how I feel

Blue Butterfly, I miss you
but I know an angel is always with me
I know God is waiting
and I know I will come back
I'm just glad I knew you
and God knows me

Blue butterfly, angel, Jesus, God
I thank you for being